Hippocrene
CHILDREN'S
ILLUSTRATED
SPANISH
DICTIONARY

ENGLISH · SPANISH
SPANISH · ENGLISH

Compiled and translated by the Editors of Hippocrene Books

Proofreading and Spanish language consultation: Ana Hernandez-Grein

Interior illustrations by S. Grant (24, 81, 88); J. Gress (page 10, 21, 24, 37, 46, 54, 59, 65, 72, 75, 77);
K. Migliorelli (page 13, 14, 18, 19, 20, 21, 22, 25, 31, 32, 37, 39, 40, 46, 47, 66, 71, 75, 76, 82, 86, 87);
B. Swidzinska (page 9, 11, 12, 13, 14, 16, 23, 27, 28, 30, 32, 33, 35, 37, 38, 41, 42, 45, 46, 47, 48, 49, 50,
52, 53, 56, 57, 58, 59, 60, 61, 62, 63, 66, 68, 69, 70, 71, 72, 73, 75, 77, 78, 79, 83), N. Zhukov (page 8, 13,
14, 17, 18, 23, 27, 29, 33, 34, 39, 40, 41, 52, 64, 65, 71, 72, 73, 78, 84, 86, 88).

Design, prepress, and production: Graafiset International, Inc.

Copyright © 1999 by Hippocrene Books, Inc.

Cataloging-in-Publication Data available from the Library of Congress.

ISBN 0-7818-0733-6

Printed in Hong Kong.

For information, address:
Hippocrene Books, Inc.
171 Madison Avenue
New York, NY 10016

INTRODUCTION

With their absorbent minds, infinite curiosities and excellent memories, children have enormous capacities to master many languages. All they need is exposure and encouragement.

The easiest way to learn a foreign language is to simulate the same natural method by which a child learns English. The natural technique is built on the concept that language is representational of concrete objects and ideas. The use of pictures and words are the natural way for children to begin to acquire a new language.

The concept of this Illustrated Dictionary is to allow children to build vocabulary and initial competency naturally. Looking at the pictorial content of the Dictionary and saying and matching the words in connection to the drawings gives children the opportunity to discover the foreign language and thus, a new way to communicate.

The drawings in the Dictionary are designed to capture children's imaginations and make the learning process interesting and entertaining, as children return to a word and picture repeatedly until they begin to recognize it.

The beautiful images and clear presentation make this dictionary a wonderful tool for unlocking your child's multilingual potential.

Deborah Dumont, M.A., M.Ed.,
Child Psychologist and Educational Consultant

Spanish Pronunciation

Letter(s)	Pronunciation system used
a	**ah** as in English 'art'
ai/ay	**igh** as in English 'high'
b	**b** as in English 'bent'
c	**k** as in English 'kitten'
ci	**see** as in English 'see'
ch	**ch** as in English 'cheese'
cua	**qu** as in English 'quarrel'
cue	**que** as in English 'quench"
d	**d** as in English 'dog'
e	**eh** as in English 'leg'
er	**air** as in English 'hair'
f	**f** as in English 'father'
g	**g** as in English 'goat'
	j as in English 'jewel'
	h as in English 'ham'
h	most often silent, sometimes a *h*-sound
i	**ee** as in English 'meet'
j	**j** as in English 'jewel'
ju	**hoo** as in English 'hoof'
k	**k** as in English 'kitten'
l	**l** as in English 'lemon'
ll	**y** as in English 'yes'
m	**m** as in English 'man'
n	**n** as in English 'new'
ña	**nya** as in the name 'Tonya'
ño	**nyo** as in 'El Niño'

Letter(s)	Pronunciation system used
o	**o** as in English 'row'
p	**p** as in English 'pan'
qu	**k** as in English 'kitten'
r	**r** as in English 'rabbit'
rr	longer, sustained *r* (rolled *r*)
s	**s** as in English 'sing'
t	**t** as in English 'tall'
u	**oo** as in English 'broom'
ue	**weh** like the *wh* in English 'when'
v	**v** as in English 'violet'
w	**w** as in English 'water'
y	**ee** as in English 'free'
z	**s** as in English 'sand'

airplane   **(el) avión**
(ehl) ah-vee-yohn

alligator   **(el) caimán**
(ehl) kigh-mahn

alphabet   **(el) alfabeto**
(ehl) al-fah-beh-to

antelope   **(el) antílope**
(ehl) an-tee-loh-peh

antlers   **(las) astas**
(lahs) ah-stas

apple   **(la) manzana**
(lah) man-sah-na

aquarium   **(el) acuario**
(ehl) ah-qua-ree-o

arch   **(el) arco**
(ehl) ar-ko

arrow   **(la) flecha**
(lah) fleh-cha

autumn   **(el) otoño**
(ehl) oh-ton-yo

baby   **(el) bebé**
(ehl) beh-beh

backpack   **(la) mochila**
(lah) mo-chee-lah

badger   **(el) tejón**
(ehl) teh-hon

baker   **(el) panadero**
(ehl) pa-na-deh-ro

ball   **(la) pelota**
(lah) peh-lo-tah

balloon   **(el) globo**
(ehl) glo-bo

banana   **(el) plátano**
(ehl) plah-ta-no

barley   **(la) cebada**
(lah) seh-ba-da

barrel   **(el) barril**
(ehl) bahr-reel

basket   **(el) cesto**
(ehl) seh-sto

bat   **(el) murciélago**
(ehl) moor-see-eh-lah-go

beach   **(la) playa**
(lah) pligh-ya

bear   **(el) oso**
(ehl) oh-so

beaver   **(el) castor**
(ehl) kah-stor

bed   **(la) cama**
(lah) kah-ma

bee   **(la) abeja**
(lah) ah-beh-hah

beetle   **(el) escarabajo**
(ehl) ehs-car-a-bah-ho

bell   **(la) campana**
(lah) kam-pah-na

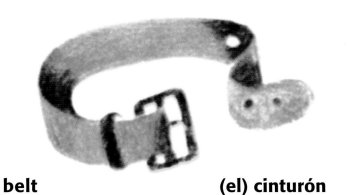

belt (el) cinturón
(ehl) seen-too-rohn

bench (el) banco
(ehl) ban-ko

bicycle (la) bicicleta
(lah) bee-see-kleh-ta

binoculars (los) gemelos
(lohs) hem-eh-los

bird (el) pájaro
(ehl) pah-ha-ro

birdcage (la) jaula
(lah) howl-a

black   **(el) negro**
(ehl) neh-gro

blossom   **(la) flor**
(lah) flohr

boat   **(el) barco**
(ehl) bar-ko

blocks   **(los) bloques**
(los) blo-kehs

blue   **(el) azul**
(ehl) ah-sool

bone   **(el) hueso**
(ehl) hweh-so

book   **(el) libro**
(ehl) lee-bro

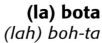

boot   **(la) bota**
(lah) boh-ta

bottle   **(la) botella**
(lah) bo-teh-ya

bowl   **(la) escudilla**
(lah) eh-skoo-dee-ya

boy   **(el) niño**
(ehl) neen-yo

bracelet   **(el) brazalete**
(ehl) bra-sa-leh-teh

branch   **(la) rama**
(lah) rah-ma

bread   **(el) pan**
(ehl) pahn

breakfast   **(el) desayuno**
(ehl) deh-sigh-oo-no

bridge   **(el) puente**
(ehl) poo-ehn-teh

broom   **(el) escoba**
(ehl) ehs-ko-ba

brother   **(el) hermano**
(ehl) air-mah-no

brown **(el) pardo**
(ehl) pahr-do

brush **(el) cepillo**
(ehl) seh-pee-yo

bucket **(el) cubo**
(ehl) koo-bo

bulletin board

(la) tablilla de anuncios
(lah) tah-blee-ya de anun-see-oz

bumblebee **(el) abejorro**
(ehl) ah-beh-hor-ro

butterfly **(la) mariposa**
(lah) mah-ree-po-sa

cab   **(el) taxi**
(ehl) tak-see

cabbage   **(la) col**
(lah) col

cactus   **(el) cacto**
(ehl) kak-to

café   **(el) café**
(ehl) kah-feh

cake   **(el) pastel**
(ehl) pah-stel

camel   **(el) camello**
(ehl) kah-meh-yo

camera (la) cámara
(lah) ka-ma-ra

candle (la) vela
(lah) veh-la

candy (el) caramelo
(ehl) ka-ra-me-lo

canoe (la) canoa
(lah) kah-no-a

cap (la) gorra
(lah) gor-ra

captain (el) capitán
(ehl) kah-pee-tan

Cc

car   **(el) coche**
(ehl) ko-cheh

card   **(la) carta**
(lah) kar-ta

carpet   **(el) alfombra**
(ehl) ahl-fom-bra

carrot   **(la) zanahoria**
(lah) zah-na-ho-ree-a

(to) carry   **llevar**
yeh-vahr

castle   **(el) castillo**
(ehl) ka-stee-yo

cat   **(el) gato**
                     (ehl) gah-to

cave   **(la) cueva**
                     (lah) queh-va

chair   **(la) silla**
                     (lah) see-ya

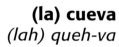

cheese   **(el) queso**
                     (ehl) keh-so

cherry   **(la) cereza**
                     (lah) seh-reh-sa

chimney   **(la) chimenea**
                     (lah) chee-men-eh-ya

chocolate   **(el) chocolate**
(ehl) cho-ko-lah-teh

Christmas tree   **(el) árbol de Navidad**
(ehl) ahr-bol deh nah-vee-dad

circus   **(el) circo**
(ehl) seer-ko

(to) climb   **subir**
soo-beer

cloud   **(la) nube**
(lah) nu-beh

clown   **(el) payaso**
(ehl) pigh-ah-so

coach   **(el) carro**
(ehl) kar-ro

coat   **(el) abrigo**
(ehl) ah-bree-go

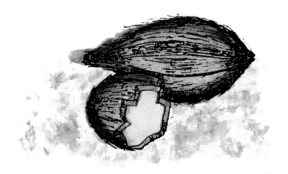

coconut   **(el) coco**
(ehl) ko-ko

comb   **(el) peine**
(ehl) peh-neh

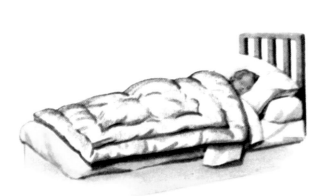

comforter   **(el) edredón**
(ehl) eh-dreh-don

compass   **(la) brujula**
(lah) broo-hoo-la

(to) cook　　　**cocinar**
ko-see-nahr

cork　　　**(el) corcho**
(ehl) kor-cho

corn　　　**(el) máiz**
(ehl) ma-ees

cow　　　**(la) vaca**
(lah) vah-ca

cracker　　　**(la) galleta**
(lah) ga-yeh-ta

cradle　　　**(la) cuna**
(lah) koo-na

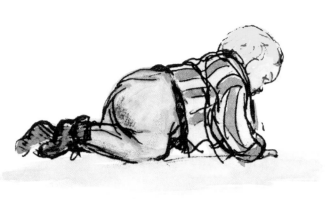

(to) crawl   **gatear**
gah-teh-ahr

(to) cross   **cruzar**
kroo-sahr

crown   **(la) corona**
(lah) ko-roh-na

(to) cry   **llorar**
yo-rahr

cucumber   **(el) pepino**
(ehl) peh-pee-no

curtain   **(la) cortina**
(lah) kor-tee-na

Dd

(to) dance **bailar**
bigh-lahr

dandelion **(el) diente de león**
(ehl) dee-en-teh deh leh-ohn

date **(la) fecha**
(lah) feh-cha

deer **(el) venado**
(ehl) veh-na-do

desert **(el) desierto**
(ehl) deh-see-air-to

desk **(el) escritorio**
(ehl) eh-skree-to-ree-oh

dirty **sucio**
soo-see-oh

dog **(el) perro**
(ehl) pehr-ro

doghouse **(la) perrera**
(lah) pehr-re-ra

doll **(la) muñeca**
(lah) moon-yeh-ka

dollhouse **(la) casa de muñecas**
(lah) kah-sa deh moon-yeh-kas

dolphin **(el) delfín**
(ehl) dehl-feen

donkey **(el) burro**
(ehl) boor-ro

dragon **(el) dragón**
(ehl) dra-gohn

dragonfly   **(la) libélula**
(lah) lee-beh-loo-la

(to) draw   **dibujar**
dee-boo-hahr

dress   **(el) vestido**
(ehl) veh-stee-do

(to) drink   **beber**
beh-bair

drum   **(el) tambor**
(ehl) tam-bor

duck   **(el) pato**
(ehl) pah-to

eagle **(la) águila**
(ehl) ah-gwee-la

(to) eat comer
ko-mair

egg **(el) huevo**
(ehl) hweh-vo

eggplant **(la) berenjena**
(lah) beh-ren-heh-na

eight ocho
oh-cho

elbow **(el) codo**
(ehl) ko-do

elephant **(el) elefante**
(ehl) eh-leh-fan-teh

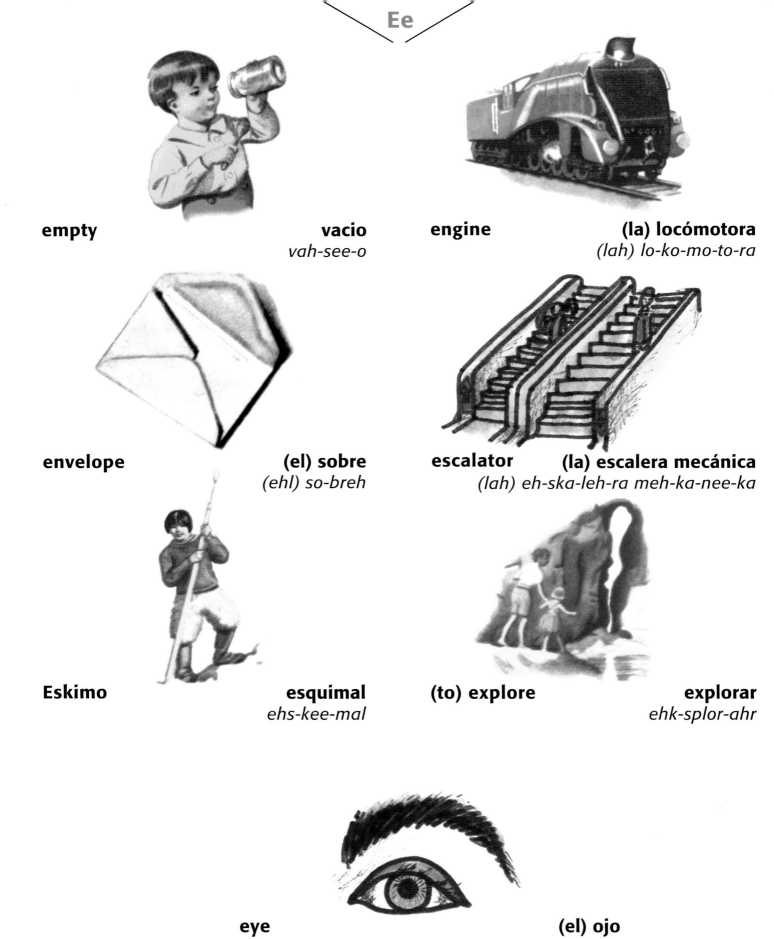

empty   **vacio**
vah-see-o

engine   **(la) locómotora**
(lah) lo-ko-mo-to-ra

envelope   **(el) sobre**
(ehl) so-breh

escalator   **(la) escalera mecánica**
(lah) eh-ska-leh-ra meh-ka-nee-ka

Eskimo   **esquimal**
ehs-kee-mal

(to) explore   **explorar**
ehk-splor-ahr

eye   **(el) ojo**
(ehl) oh-jo

face   **(la) cara**
(lah) ka-ra

fan   **(el) ventilador**
(ehl) ven-tee-lah-dor

father   **(el) padre**
(ehl) pah-dreh

fear   **(el) miedo**
(ehl) mee-eh-do

feather   **(la) pluma**
(lah) ploo-ma

(to) feed   **alimentar**
ah-lee-men-tahr

fence   **(la) cerca**
(lah) sair-ka

fern   **(el) helecho**
(ehl) eh-leh-cho

field   **(el) campo**
(ehl) kam-po

field mouse   **(el) ratón de campo**
(ehl) rah-ton deh kahm-po

finger   **(el) dedo**
(ehl) deh-do

fir tree   **(el) abeto**
(ehl) ah-beh-to

fire　**(el) fuego**
(ehl) fweh-go

fish　**(el) pez**
(ehl) pehz

(to) fish　**pescar**
pe-skahr

fist　**(el) puño**
(ehl) poo-nyo

five　**cinco**
seen-ko

flag　**(la) bandera**
(lah) ban-dair-a

flashlight   **(la) linterna eléctrica**
(lah) leen-tair-na eh-lek-tree-ka

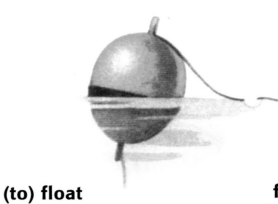

(to) float   **flotar**
flo-tahr

flower   **(la) flor**
(lah) flor

(to) fly   **volar**
vo-lahr

foot   **(el) pie**
(ehl) pee-eh

fork   **(el) tenedor**
(ehl) teh-ne-dor

fountain   **(la) fuente**
(lah) fwehn-teh

four **cuatro**
quah-tro

fox **(el) zorro**
(ehl) zor-ro

frame **(el) marco**
(ehl) mar-ko

friend **(el) amigo**
(ehl) ah-mee-go

frog **(la) rana**
(lah) rah-na

fruit **(la) fruta**
(lah) froo-ta

furniture **(los) muebles**
(lohs) mweh-blehs

garden   **(el) jardín**
(ehl) har-deen

gate   **(la) cerca**
(lah) ser-ka

(to) gather   **coger**
ko-hair

geranium   **(el) geranio**
(ehl) he-rah-nee-o

giraffe   **(la) jirafa**
(lah) hee-ra-fa

girl   **(la) niña**
(lah) neen-ya

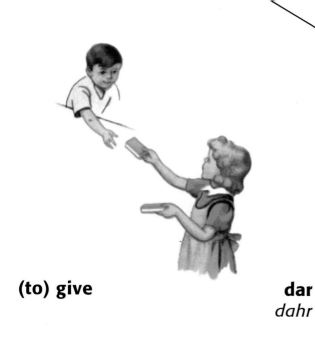

(to) give　　　　**dar**
dahr

glass　　　　**(el) vaso**
(ehl) vah-so

glasses　　　　**(las) gafas**
(lahs) gah-fas

globe　　　　**(la) esfera**
(lah) es-feh-ra

glove　　　　**(el) guante**
(ehl) gwan-teh

goat　　　　**(la) cabra**
(lah) kah-bra

goldfish **(el) pez de colores**
(ehl) pays deh ko-lo-rehs

"Good Night" **Buenas noches**
bweh-nahs no-chehs

"Good-bye" **Adiós**
ah-dee-os

goose **(el) ganso**
(ehl) gahn-so

grandfather **(el) abuelo**
(ehl) ah-bweh-lo

grandmother **(la) abuela**
(lah) ah-bweh-la

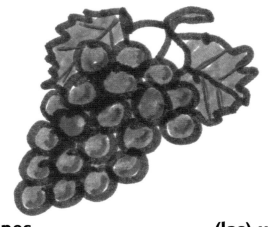

grapes **(las) uvas**
(lahs) oo-vas

grasshopper **(el) saltamontes**
(ehl) sal-ta-mon-tehs

green **(el) verde**
(ehl) vair-deh

greenhouse **(el) invernadero**
(ehl) een-vair-na-de-ro

guitar **(la) guitarra**
(lah) gee-tahr-ra

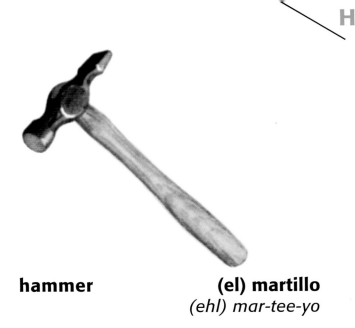

hammer **(el) martillo**
(ehl) mar-tee-yo

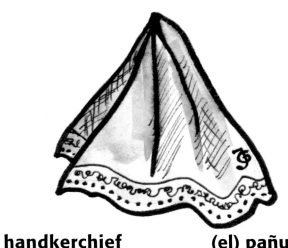

hammock **(la) hamaca**
(lah) hah-ma-ka

hamster **(el) hamster**
(ehl) ham-stair

hand **(la) mano**
(lah) mah-no

handbag **(el) bolso**
(ehl) bol-so

handkerchief **(el) pañuelo**
(ehl) pan-oo-eh-lo

harvest   **(la) cosecha**
(lah) ko-seh-cha

hat   **(el) sombrero**
(ehl) som-breh-ro

hay   **(el) heno**
(ehl) eh-no

headdress   **(el) tocado de plumas**
(ehl) to-kah-do deh plu-mas

heart   **(el) corazón**
(ehl) kor-ah-sohn

hedgehog   **(el) erizo**
(ehl) air-ee-so

hen   **(la) gallina**
(lah) ga-yee-na

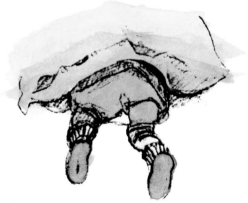

(to) hide   **esconder**
ehs-kon-dair

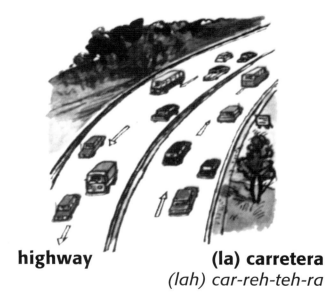

highway   **(la) carretera**
(lah) car-reh-teh-ra

honey   **(la) miel**
(lah) mee-el

horns   **(los) cuernos**
(lohs) quehr-nos

horse   **(el) caballo**
(ehl) ka-bah-yo

horseshoe **(la) herradura**
(lah) air-ra-doo-ra

hourglass **(el) reloj de arena**
(ehl) reh-loh deh ah-rain-a

house **(la) casa**
(lah) kah-sa

(to) hug **abrazar**
ah-bra-sahr

hydrant **(la) boca de riego**
(lah) bo-ka deh ree-eh-go

li

ice cream **(el) helado**
(ehl) eh-lah-do

ice cubes **(los) cubitos de hielo**
(los) koo-bee-tos deh ee-yeh-lo

ice-skating **patinar**
pah-tee-nar

instrument **(el) instrumento**
(ehl) een-stroo-men-to

iris **(el) iris**
(ehl) eer-ees

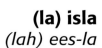

iron **(la) plancha** **island** **(la) isla**
(lah) plan-cha *(lah) ees-la*

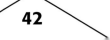

jacket **(la) chaqueta**
(lah) cha-keh-ta

jam **(la) mermelada**
(lah) mer-meh-la-da

jigsaw puzzle **(el) rompecabezas**
(ehl) rom-peh-ka-beh-sas

jockey **(el) jockey**
(ehl) jaw-kee

juggler **(el) malabarista**
(ehl) ma-la-ba-ree-sta

(to) jump **saltar**
sal-tahr

kangaroo　　**(el) canguro**
(ehl) kan-goo-ro

key　　**(la) llave**
(lah) yah-veh

kitten　　**(el) gatito**
(ehl) gah-tee-to

knife　　**(el) cuchillo**
(ehl) koo-chee-yo

knight　　**(el) caballero**
(ehl) kah-ba-yeh-ro

(to) knit　　**tejer**
teh-hair

knot　　**(el) nudo**
(ehl) noo-do

koala bear　　**(la) koala**
(lah) ko-ah-la

ladder   **(la) escala**
(lah) eh-skah-la

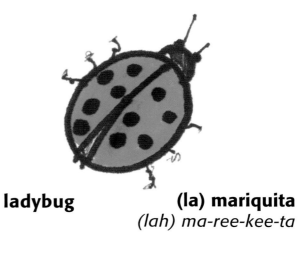

ladybug   **(la) mariquita**
(lah) ma-ree-kee-ta

lamb   **(el) cordero**
(ehl) kor-dair-o

lamp   **(la) lámpara**
(lah) lahm-pa-ra

(to) lap   **lamer**
lah-mair

laughter   **(la) risa**
(lah) ree-sa

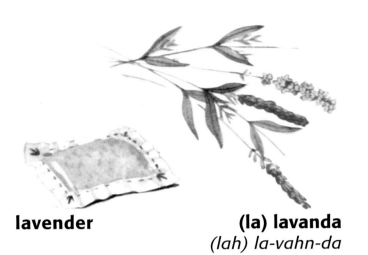

lavender   **(la) lavanda**
                   (lah) la-vahn-da

lawn mower   **(el) cortacésped**
                   (ehl) kor-ta-ses-ped

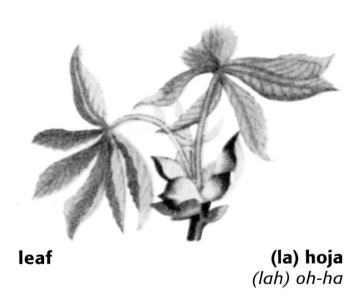

leaf   **(la) hoja**
                   (lah) oh-ha

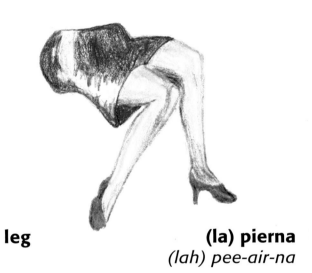

leg   **(la) pierna**
                   (lah) pee-air-na

lemon   **(el) limón**
                   (ehl) lee-mohn

lettuce   **(la) lechuga**
                   (lah) leh-choo-ga

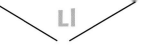

lightbulb **(la) bombilla**
(lah) bom-bee-ya

lighthouse **(el) faro**
(ehl) fah-ro

lilac **(la) lila**
(lah) lee-la

lion **(el) león**
(ehl) leh-ohn

(to) listen **escuchar**
ehs-koo-chahr

lobster **(la) langosta**
(lah) lan-go-sta

lock   **(la) cerradura**
(lah) sehr-rah-doo-ra

lovebirds   **(los) periquitos**
(lohs) peh-ri-kee-tos

luggage   **(las) maletas**
(lahs) ma-leh-tas

lumberjack   **(el) leñador**
(ehl) len-ya-dor

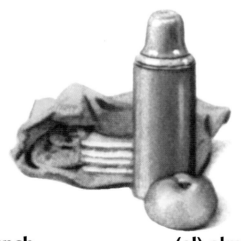

lunch   **(el) almuerzo**
(ehl) ahl-mwehr-so

lynx   **(el) lince**
(ehl) leen-seh

magazine **(la) revista**
(lah) reh-vee-sta

magician **(el) ilusionista**
(ehl) ee-loo-see-on-ee-sta

magnet **(el) imán**
(ehl) ee-man

map **(el) mapa**
(ehl) mah-pa

maple leaf **(el) arce**
(ehl) ahr-seh

marketplace **(la) plaza del mercado**
(lah) plah-sa dehl mer-ka-do

mask **(la) máscara**
(lah) mah-sca-ra

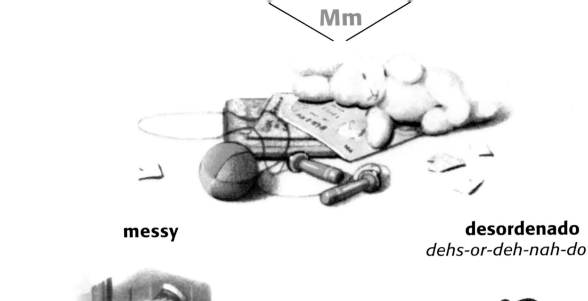

messy

desordenado
dehs-or-deh-nah-do

milkman

(el) lechero
(ehl) leh-cheh-ro

mirror

(el) espejo
(ehl) ehs-peh-ho

mitten

(el) mitón
(ehl) mee-tohn

money

(el) dinero
(ehl) dee-nair-o

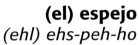

monkey

(el) mono
(ehl) mo-no

moon

(la) luna
(lah) loo-na

mother   **(la) madre**
(lah) mah-dreh

mountain   **(la) montaña**
(lah) mon-tahn-ya

mouse   **(el) ratón**
(ehl) rah-ton

mouth   **(la) boca**
(lah) boh-ka

mushroom   **(el) hongo**
(ehl) on-go

music   **(la) música**
(lah) moo-see-ka

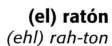

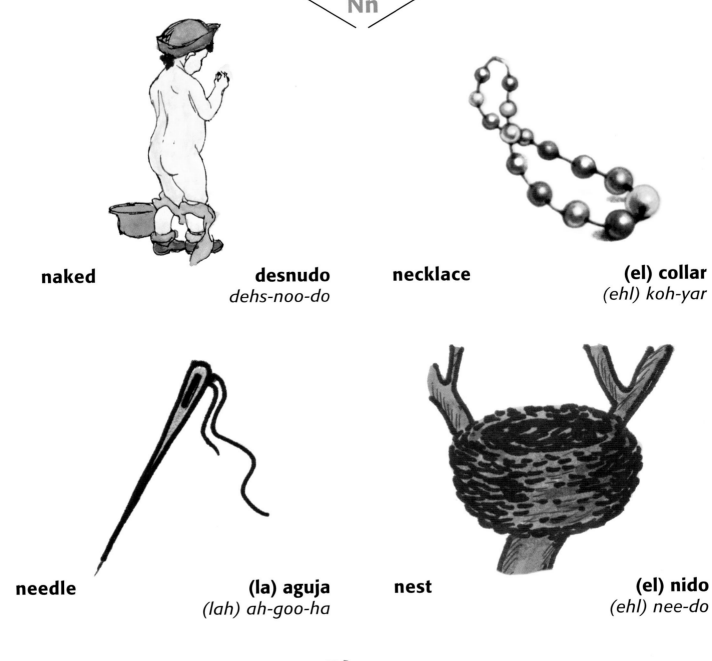

naked　　**desnudo**
dehs-noo-do

necklace　　**(el) collar**
(ehl) koh-yar

needle　　**(la) aguja**
(lah) ah-goo-ha

nest　　**(el) nido**
(ehl) nee-do

newspaper　　**(el) periódico**
(ehl) pair-ee-o-dee-ko

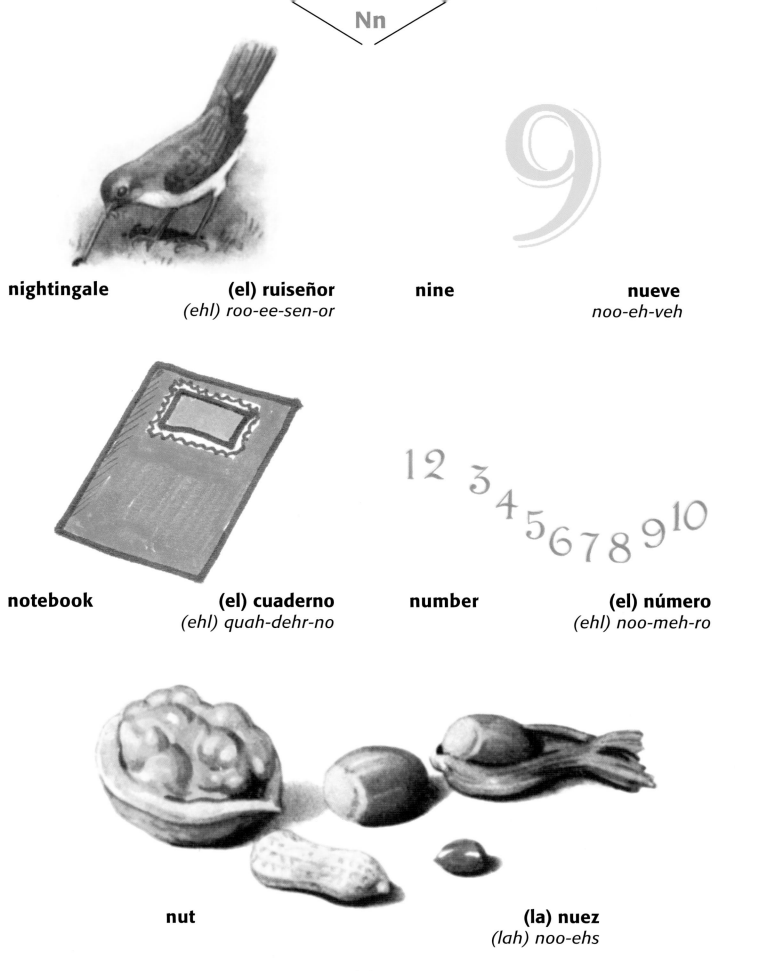

nightingale   **(el) ruiseñor**
(ehl) roo-ee-sen-or

nine   **nueve**
noo-eh-veh

notebook   **(el) cuaderno**
(ehl) quah-dehr-no

number   **(el) número**
(ehl) noo-meh-ro

nut   **(la) nuez**
(lah) noo-ehs

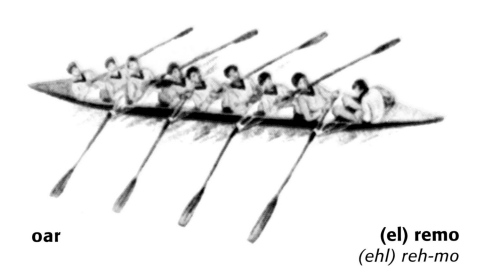

oar   **(el) remo**
(ehl) reh-mo

ocean liner   **(el) buque transoceánico**   **old**   **viejo**
(ehl) boo-keh trans-o-see-ahn-ee-ko   *vee-eh-ho*

1

one   **uno**   **onion**   **(la) cebolla**
oo-no   *(lah) seh-boh-ya*

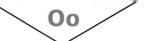

open **abierto**
ah-bee-air-to

orange **(la) naranja**
(lah) na-ran-ha

ostrich **(el) avestruz**
(ehl) ah-veh-stroos

owl **(la) lechuza**
(lah) leh-chu-za

ox **(el) buey**
(ehl) boo-ay

padlock   **(el) candado**
(ehl) kan-dah-do

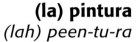

paint   **(la) pintura**
(lah) peen-tu-ra

painter   **(el) pintor**
(ehl) peen-tor

pajamas   **(las) pijamas**
(lahs) pee-jam-as

palm tree   **(la) palma**
(lah) pal-ma

paper   **(el) papel**
(ehl) pah-pel

parachute   **(el) paracaídas**
(ehl) pah-ra-kigh-das

park   **(el) parque**
(ehl) par-keh

parrot   **(el) loro**
(ehl) loh-ro

passport   **(el) pasaporte**
(ehl) pas-a-por-teh

patch   **(el) remiendo**
(ehl) reh-mee-en-do

path   **(el) camino**
(ehl) kah-mee-no

peach   **(el) melocotón**
(ehl) mel-o-ko-ton

pear   **(la) pera**
(lah) peh-ra

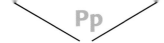

pebble

(la) china
(lah) chee-na

(to) peck　　　　**picotear**
pee-ko-teh-ahr

(to) peel　　　　**pelar**
peh-lahr

pelican　　　　**(el) pelicano**
(ehl) pel-ee-ka-no

pencil　　　　**(el) lapiz**
(ehl) lah-pees

penguin　　　　**(el) pingüino**
(ehl) peen-gwee-no

people　　　　**(la) gente**
(lah) hen-teh

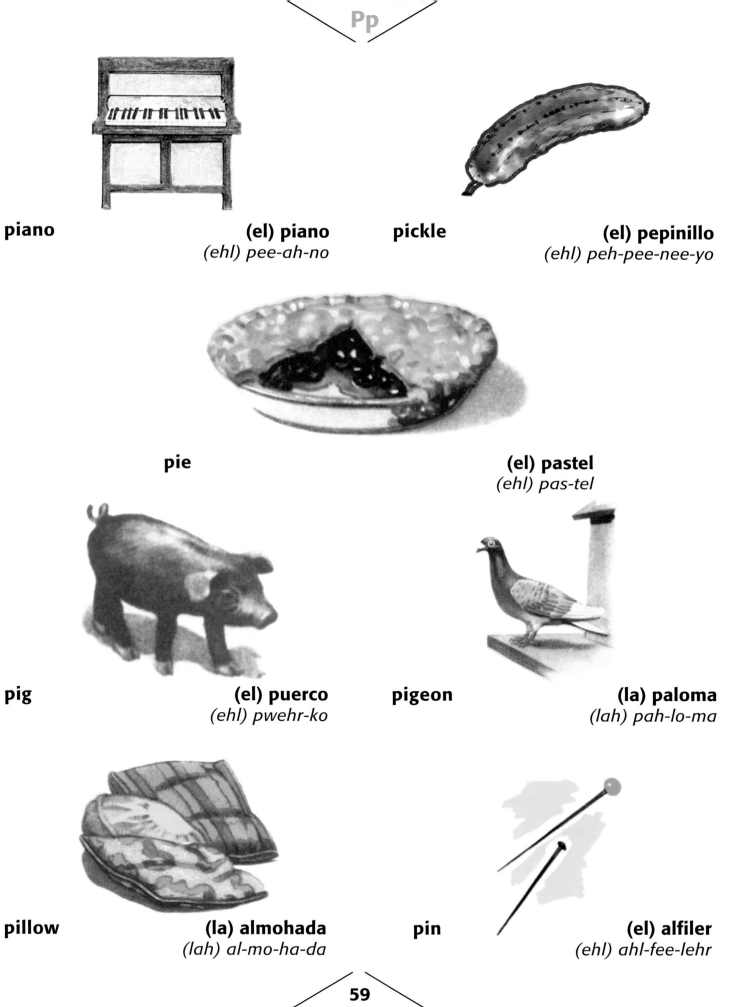

piano **(el) piano**
(ehl) pee-ah-no

pickle **(el) pepinillo**
(ehl) peh-pee-nee-yo

pie **(el) pastel**
(ehl) pas-tel

pig **(el) puerco**
(ehl) pwehr-ko

pigeon **(la) paloma**
(lah) pah-lo-ma

pillow **(la) almohada**
(lah) al-mo-ha-da

pin **(el) alfiler**
(ehl) ahl-fee-lehr

pine **(el) pino**
(ehl) pee-no

pineapple **(la) piña**
(lah) peen-ya

pit **(el) hoyo**
(ehl) oy-yo

pitcher **(el) jarro**
(ehl) jahr-ro

plate **(el) plato**
(ehl) plah-to

platypus **(el) platypus**
(ehl) plah-tee-poos

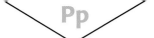

(to) play **jugar**
hoo-gahr

plum **(la) ciruela**
(lah) see-roo-eh-la

polar bear **(el) oso polar**
(ehl) oh-so po-lar

pony **(el) caballito**
(ehl) kah-bai-yee-to

pot **(la) olla**
(lah) oh-ya

potato **(la) papa**
(lah) pah-pa

(to) pour   **vaciar**
vah-see-ahr

present   **(el) regalo**
(ehl) reh-ga-lo

(to) pull   **halar**
ah-lahr

pumpkin   **(la) calabaza**
(lah) kal-a-bah-sa

puppy   **(el) perrito**
(ehl) pehr-ree-to

queen   **(la) reina**
(lah) reh-ee-na

rabbit

(el) conejo
(ehl) ko-neh-ho

raccoon

(el) mapache
(ehl) ma-pah-cheh

racket

(la) raqueta
(lah) rah-keh-ta

radio

(el) radio
(ehl) rah-dee-o

radish

(el) rábano
(ehl) rah-ba-no

raft   **(la) balsa**
(lah) bal-sa

rain   **(la) lluvia**
(lah) yoo-vee-a

rainbow   **(el) arco iris**
(ehl) ar-ko eer-ees

raincoat   **(el) impermeable**
(ehl) een-pair-mee-ah-bleh

raspberry   **(la) frambuesa**
(lah) fram-bweh-sa

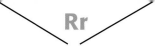

(to) read　　　　**leer**
leh-air

red　　　**(el) rojo**
(ehl) ro-ho

refrigerator　　　**(el) refrigerador**
(ehl) reh-freh-her-ah-dor

rhinoceros　　　**(el) rinoceronte**
(ehl) ree-no-sair-an-teh

ring　　　**(el) anillo**
(ehl) ah-nee-yo

(to) ring   **sonar**
so-nahr

river   **(el) río**
(ehl) ree-o

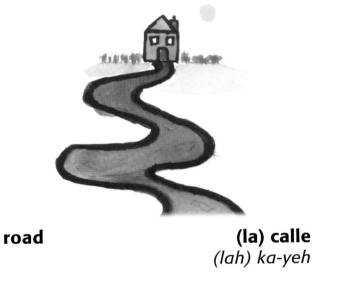

road   **(la) calle**
(lah) ka-yeh

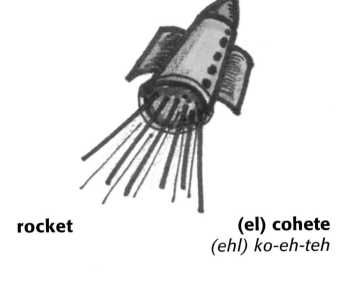

rocket   **(el) cohete**
(ehl) ko-eh-teh

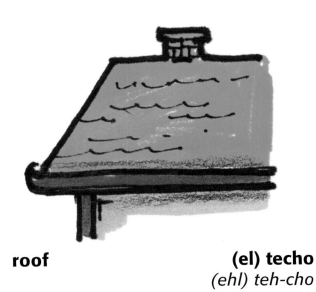

roof   **(el) techo**
(ehl) teh-cho

rooster   **(el) gallo**
(ehl) gah-yo

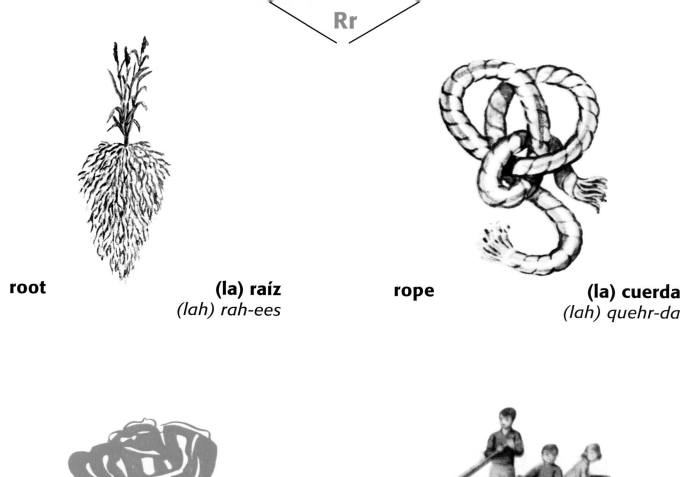

root   **(la) raíz**
(lah) rah-ees

rope   **(la) cuerda**
(lah) quehr-da

rose   **(la) rosa**
(lah) ro-sa

(to) row   **remar**
reh-mahr

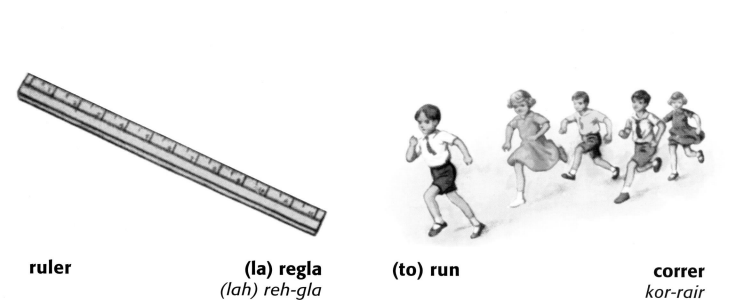

ruler   **(la) regla**
(lah) reh-gla

(to) run   **correr**
kor-rair

safety pin **(el) imperdible**
(ehl) eem-pehr-dee-ble

(to) sail **navegar**
nah-veh-gahr

sailor **(el) marinero**
(ehl) mar-ee-neh-ro

salt **(la) sal**
(lah) sal

scarf **(la) bufanda**
(lah) boo-fahn-da

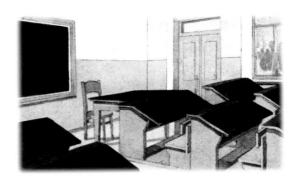

school **(la) escuela**
(lah) ehs-koo-eh-la

scissors **(las) tijeras**
(lahs) tee-ehr-as

screwdriver **(el) destornillador**
(ehl) dehs-tor-nee-ya-dor

seagull **(la) gaviota**
(lah) gah-vee-o-ta

seesaw **(el) balancín**
(ehl) bal-an-seen

seven **siete**
see-eh-teh

(to) sew **coser**
ko-sair

shark   **(el) tiburón**
(ehl) tee-boo-ron

sheep   **(la) oveja**
(lah) oh-veh-hah

shell   **(la) concha**
(lah) kohn-chah

shepherd   **(el) pastor**
(ehl) pahs-tohr

ship   **(el) barco**
(ehl) bahr-koh

shirt   **(la) camisa**
(lah) kah-mee-sah

shoe   **(el) zapato**
(ehl) sah-pah-toh

shovel   **(la) pala**
(lah) pah-lah

(to) show   **mostrar**
moh-strahr

shower   **(la) ducha**
(lah) doo-cha

shutter   **(la) contraventana**
(lah) kohn-trah-vehn-ta-nah

sick   **enfermo**
ehn-fair-moh

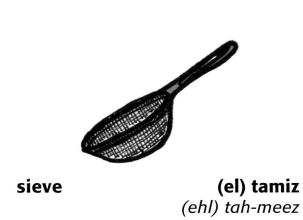

sieve   **(el) tamiz**
(ehl) tah-meez

(to) sing   **cantar**
kahn-tahr

(to) sit   **sentar(se)**
sehn-tahr (seh)

six   **seis**
sai-s

sled   **(el) trineo**
(ehl) tree-neh-oh

(to) sleep   **dormir**
dohr-meer

small

pequeño
peh-keh-nyoh

smile

(la) sonrisa
(lah) sohn-ree-sah

snail

(el) caracol
(ehl) kah-rah-kohl

snake

(el) serpiente
(ehl) sehr-pee-ehn-teh

snow

(la) nieve
(lah) nee-eh-veh

sock

(el) calcetín
(ehl) kahl-seh-teen

sofa   **(la) sofa**
(lah) soh-fah

sparrow   **(el) gorrión**
(ehl) gohr-ree-ohn

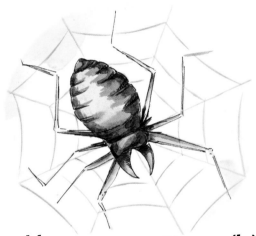

spider   **(la) araña**
(lah) ah-rahn-yah

spiderweb   **(la) tela de araña**
(lah) teh-lah deh ah-rahn-yah

spoon   **(la) cuchara**
(lah) koo-chah-rah

squirrel   **(la) ardilla**
(lah) ahr-dee-yah

stairs　　　　　**(la) escalera**
(lah) eh-ska-le-ra

stamp　　　　　**(la) estampa**
(lah) eh-stam-pa

starfish　　　**(la) estrella de mar**
(lah) eh-streh-ya deh mahr

stork　　　　　**(la) cigüeña**
(lah) see-gwehn-yah

stove　　　　　**(la) estufa**
(lah) eh-stoo-fah

strawberry　　　　**(la) fresa**
(lah) freh-sah

subway　　　　　**(el) metro**
(ehl) meh-troh

sugar cube　**(el) cubito de azucar**
(ehl) koo-bee-toh deh ah-soo-kahr

sun　　　　　**(el) sol**
(ehl) sol

sunflower　　　**(el) girasol**
(ehl) gee-rah-sol

sweater　　　　**(el) suéter**
(ehl) sweh-tehr

(to) sweep　　　**barrer**
bahr-rair

swing　　　　**(el) columpio**
(ehl) ko-loom-pi-o

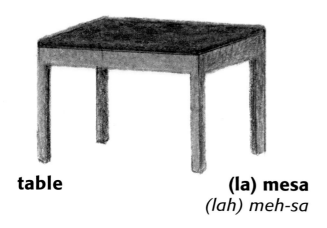

table **(la) mesa**
(lah) meh-sa

teapot **(la) tetera**
(lah) teh-te-rah

teddy bear **(el) oso de juguete**
(ehl) oh-soh deh hoo-geh-teh

television **(el) televisor**
(ehl) tehl-eh-vee-sor

ten **diez**
dee-ehs

tent **(la) tienda de campaña**
(lah) tee-yen-dah deh cam-pahn-yah

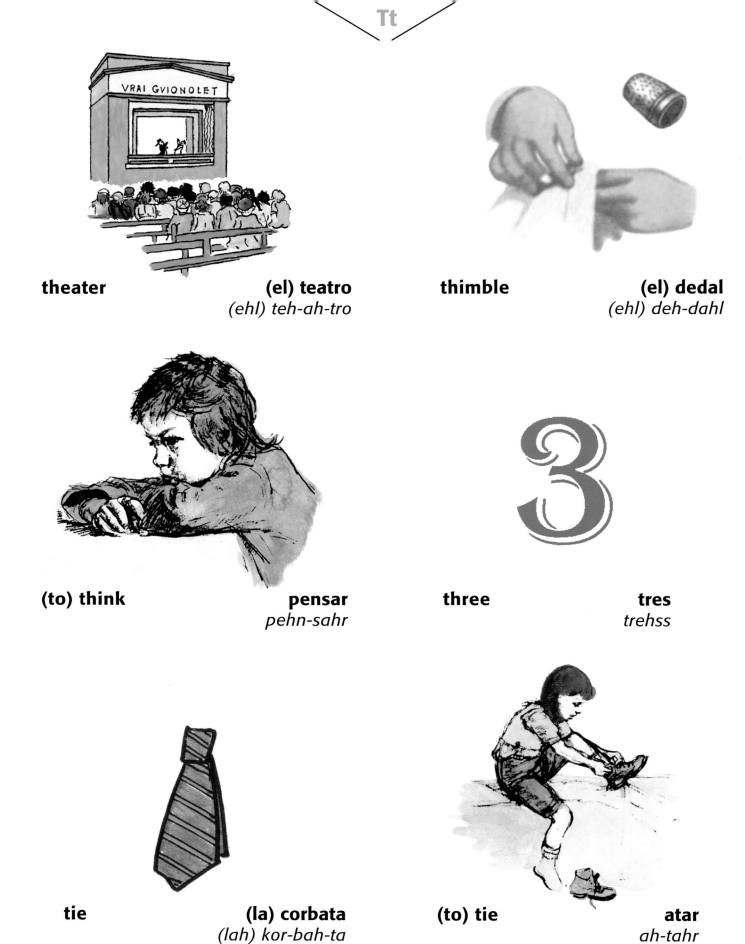

theater   **(el) teatro**
(ehl) teh-ah-tro

thimble   **(el) dedal**
(ehl) deh-dahl

(to) think   **pensar**
pehn-sahr

three   **tres**
trehss

tie   **(la) corbata**
(lah) kor-bah-ta

(to) tie   **atar**
ah-tahr

tiger **(el) tigre**
(ehl) tee-greh

toaster **(lah) tostadora**
(lah) tos-tah-do-ra

tomato **(el) tomate**
(ehl) toh-mah-teh

toucan **(el) tucan**
(ehl) too-kan

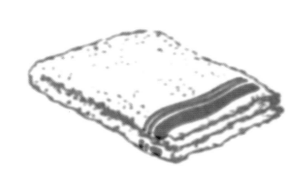

towel **(la) toalla**
(lah) to-ah-yah

tower **(la) torre**
(lah) tohr-reh

toy box   **(la) caja de juguetes**
(lah) ka-ja de hoo-geh-tes

tracks   **(la) pista**
(lah) pees-ta

train station   **(la) estación del tren**
(lah) eh-sta-see-on dehl train

tray   **(la) bandeja**
(lah) bahn-deh-hah

tree   **(el) árbol**
(ehl) ahr-bol

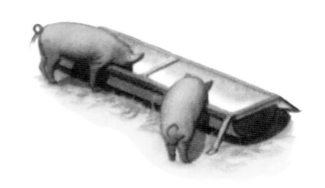

trough   **(el) abrevadero**
(ehl) ah-breh-vah-deh-roh

truck

(el) camión
(ehl) cah-mee-yohn

trumpet   **(la) trompeta**
(lah) trom-peh-tah

tulip   **(el) tulipán**
(ehl) too-leh-pahn

tunnel   **(el) túnel**
(ehl) toon-ehl

turtle   **(la) tortuga**
(lah) tohr-too-ga

twins   **(los) gemelos**
(lohs) heh-meh-lohs

two   **dos**
dohs

umbrella **(el) paraguas**
(ehl) par-ah-gwahs

uphill **ascendente**
ah-sen-den-teh

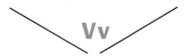

Vv

vase **(el) vaso**
(ehl) vah-soh

veil **(el) velo**
(ehl) veh-loh

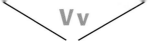

village

(el) pueblo
(ehl) pweh-blo

violet
(la) violeta
(lah) vee-oh-le-ta

violin
(el) violín
(ehl) vee-oh-leen

voyage
(el) viaje
(ehl) vee-ah-heh

waiter　　　　　**(el) camarero**
(ehl) cah-ma-reh-ro

(to) wake up　　　**despertar(se)**
dehs-per-tahr (seh)

walrus　　　　　**(la) morsa**
(lah) mor-sa

(to) wash　　　　　**lavar**
lah-vahr

watch　　　　　**(el) reloj**
(ehl) reh-lo

(to) watch　　　　　**mirar**
mee-rahr

(to) water　　**regar**
reh-gahr

waterfall　　**(la) cascada**
(lah) cahs-cah-dah

watering can　　**(la) regadera**
(lah) reh-ga-deh-ra

watermelon　　**(la) sandía**
(lah) sahn-dee-yah

weather vane　　**(la) veleta**
(lah) veh-leh-tah

(to) weigh　　**pesar**
peh-sahr

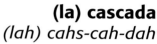

whale   **(la) ballena**
(lah) ba-yeh-na

wheel   **(la) rueda**
(lah) roo-eh-dah

wheelbarrow   **(la) carretilla**
(lah) cahr-reh-tee-yah

whiskers   **(los) bigotes**
(lohs) bee-go-tehs

(to) whisper   **susurrar**
suh-sur-rahr

whistle   **(la) chifla**
(lah) chee-flah

white **(el) blanco**
(ehl) blahn-co

wig **(la) peluca**
(lah) peh-loo-kah

wind **(el) viento**
(ehl) vee-ehn-toh

window **(la) ventana**
(lah) vehn-tah-na

wings **(la) ala**
(lah) ah-la

winter **(el) invierno**
(ehl) een-vee-air-no

wolf

(el) zorro
(ehl) sohr-ro

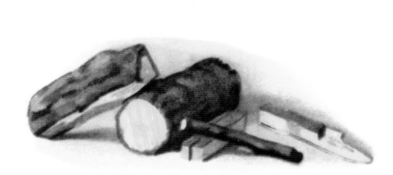

wood   **(la) madera**
(lah) ma-deh-ra

word   **(la) palabra**
(lah) pah-lah-bra

(to) write

escribir
eh-skree-beer

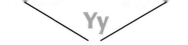

yellow   **(el) amarillo**
                          (ehl) ah-ma-ree-yo

Zz

zebra   **(la) cebra**
                          (lah) seh-bra

A

abeja (la) bee
abejorro (el) bumblebee
abeto (el) fir tree
abierto open
abrazar (to) hug
abrevadero (el) trough
abrigo (el) coat
abuela (la) grandmother
abuelo (el) grandfather
acuario (el) aquarium
Adiós Good-bye
águila (la) eagle
aguja (la) needle
ala (la) wings
alfabeto (el) alphabet
alfiler (el) pin
alfombra (el) carpet
alimentar (to) feed
almohada (la) pillow
almuerzo (el) lunch
amarillo (el) yellow
amigo (el) friend
anillo (el) ring
antílope (el) antelope
araña (la) spider
árbol (el) tree
árbol de Navidad (el)
    Christmas tree
arce (el) maple leaf
arco (el) arch
arco iris (el) rainbow
ardilla (la) squirrel
ascendente uphill
astas (las) antlers
atar (to) tie
avestruz (el) ostrich
avión (el) airplane
azul (el) blue

B

bailar (to) dance
ballena (la) whale

balsa (la) raft
banco (el) bench
bandeja (la) tray
bandera (la) flag
barco (el) boat; ship
barrer (to) sweep
barril (el) barrel
bebé (el) baby
beber (to) drink
berenjena (la) eggplant
bicicleta (la) bicycle
bigotes (los) whiskers
blanco (el) white
bloques (los) blocks
boca (la) mouth
boca de riego (la) hydrant
bolso (el) handbag
bombilla (la) lightbulb
bota (la) boot
botella (la) bottle
brazalete (el) bracelet
brujula (la) compass
Buenas noches Good Night
buey (el) ox
bufanda (la) scarf
buque transoceánico (el)
    ocean liner
burro (el) donkey

C

caballero (el) knight
caballito (el) pony
caballo (el) horse
cabra (la) goat
cacto (el) cactus
café (el) café
caimán (el) alligator
caja de juguetes (la) toy box
calabaza (la) pumpkin
calcetín (el) sock
calle (la) road
cama (la) bed
cámara (la) camera
camarero (el) waiter
camello (el) camel
camino (el) path

camión (el) truck
camisa (la) shirt
campana (la) bell
campo (el) field
candado (el) padlock
canguro (el) kangaroo
canoa (la) canoe
cantar (to) sing
capitán (el) captain
cara (la) face
caracol (el) snail
caramelo (el) candy
carretera (la) highway
carretilla (la) wheelbarrow
carro (el) coach
carta (la) card
casa (la) house
casa de muñecas (la) dollhouse
cascada (la) waterfall
castillo (el) castle
castor (el) beaver
cebada (la) barley
cebolla (la) onion
cebra (la) zebra
cepillo (el) brush
cerca (la) fence; gate
cereza (la) cherry
cerradura (la) lock
cesto (el) basket
chaqueta (la) jacket
chifla (la) whistle
chimenea (la) chimney
china (la) pebble
chocolate (el) chocolate
cigüeña (la) stork
cinco five
cinturón (el) belt
circo (el) circus
ciruela (la) plum
coche (el) car
cocinar (to) cook
coco (el) coconut
codo (el) elbow

impermeable (el) raincoat
instrumento (el) instrument
invernadero (el) greenhouse
invierno (el) winter
iris (el) iris
isla (la) island

J

jardín (el) garden
jarro (el) pitcher
jaula (la) birdcage
jirafa (la) giraffe
jockey (el) jockey
jugar (to) play

K

koala (la) koala bear

L

lamer (to) lap
lámpara (la) lamp
langosta (la) lobster
lapiz (el) pencil
lavanda (la) lavender
lavar (to) wash
lechero (el) milkman
lechuga (la) lettuce
lechuza (la) bowl
leer (to) read
leñador (el) lumberjack
león (el) lion
libélula (la) dragonfly
libro (el) book
lila (la) lilac
limón (el) lemon
lince (el) lynx
linterna eléctrica (la) flashlight
llave (la) key
llevar (to) carry
llorar (to) cry
lluvia (la) rain
locómotora (la) engine
loro (el) parrot
luna (la) moon

M

madera (la) wood
madre (la) mother
máiz (el) corn
malabarista (el) juggler
maletas (las) luggage
mano (la) hand
manzana (la) apple
mapa (el) map
mapache (el) raccoon
marco (el) frame
marinero (el) sailor
mariposa (la) butterfly
mariquita (la) ladybug
martillo (el) hammer
máscara (la) mask
melocotón (el) peach
mermelada (la) jam
mesa (la) table
metro (el) subway
miedo (el) fear
miel (la) honey
mirar (to) watch
mitón (el) mitten
mochila (la) backpack
mono (el) monkey
montaña (la) mountain
morsa (la) walrus
mostrar (to) show
muebles (los) furniture
muñeca (la) doll
murciélago (el) bat

N

naranja (la) orange
navegar (to) sail
negro (el) black
nido (el) nest
nieve (la) snow
niña (la) girl
niño (el) boy
nube (la) cloud
nudo (el) knot
nueve nine
nuez (la) nut
número (el) number

O

ocho eight
ojo (el) eye
olla (la) pot
oso (el) bear
oso de juguete (el) teddy bear
oso polar (el) polar bear
otoño (el) autumn
oveja (la) sheep

P

padre (el) father
pájaro (el) bird
pala (la) shovel
palabra (la) word
palma (la) palm tree
paloma (la) pigeon
pan (el) bread
panadero (el) baker
pañuelo (el) handkerchief
papa (la) potato
papel (el) paper
paraguas (el) umbrella
pardo (el) brown
parque (el) park
pasaporte (el) passport
pastel (el) cake; pie
pastor (el) shepherd
patinar ice-skating
pato (el) duck
payaso (el) clown
peine (el) comb
pelar (to) peel
pelicano (el) pelican
pelota (la) ball

U

uno one
uvas (las) grapes

V

vaca (la) cow
vaciar (to) pour
vacio empty
vaso (el) glass; vase
vela (la) candle
veleta (la) weather vane
velo (el) veil
venado (el) deer
ventana (la) window
ventilador (el) fan
verde (el) green
vestido (el) dress
viaje (el) voyage
viejo old
viento (el) wind
violeta (la) violet
violín (el) violin
volar (to) fly

Z

zanahoria (la) carrot
zapato (el) shoe
zorro (el) fox; wolf

Folk Tales from Bohemia
Adolf Wenig
This folk tale collection is one of a kind, focusing uniquely on humankind's struggle with evil in the world. Delicately ornate red and black text and illustrations set the mood.
Ages 9 and up
90 pages • red and black illustrations • 5 1/2 x 8 1/4 • 0-7818-0718-2 • W • $14.95hc • (786)

Czech, Moravian and Slovak Fairy Tales
Parker Fillmore
Fifteen different classic, regional folk tales and 23 charming illustrations whisk the reader to places of romance, deception, royalty, and magic.
Ages 12 and up
243 pages • 23 b/w illustrations • 5 1/2 x 8 1/4 • 0-7818-0714-X • W • $14.95 hc • (792)

Glass Mountain: Twenty-Eight Ancient Polish Folk Tales and Fables
W.S. Kuniczak
Illustrated by Pat Bargielski
As a child in a far-away misty corner of Volhynia, W.S. Kuniczak was carried away to an extraordinary world of magic and illusion by the folk tales of his Polish nurse.
171 pages • 6 x 9 • 8 illustrations • 0-7818-0552-X • W • $16.95hc • (645)

Old Polish Legends
Retold by F.C. Anstruther
Wood engravings by J. Sekalski
This fine collection of eleven fairy tales, with an introduction by Zymunt Nowakowski, was first published in Scotland during World War II.
66 pages • 7 1/4 x 9 • 11 woodcut engravings • 0-7818-0521-X • W • $11.95hc • (653)

Folk Tales from Russia
by Donald A. Mackenzie
With nearly 200 pages and 8 full-page black-and-white illustrations, the reader will be charmed by these legendary folk tales that symbolically weave magical fantasy with the historic events of Russia's past.
Ages 12 and up
192 pages • 8 b/w illustrations • 5 1/2 x 8 1/4 • 0-7818-0696-8 • W • $12.50hc • (788)

Fairy Gold: A Book of Classic English Fairy Tales
Chosen by Ernest Rhys
Illustrated by Herbert Cole
Forty-nine imaginative black and white illustrations accompany thirty classic tales, including such beloved stories as "Jack and the Bean Stalk" and "The Three Bears."
Ages 12 and up
236 pages • 5 1/2 x 8 1/4 • 49 b/w illustrations • 0-7818-0700-X • W • $14.95hc • (790)

Tales of Languedoc: From the South of France

Samuel Jacques Brun

For readers of all ages, here is a masterful collection of folk tales from the south of France.

Ages 12 and up

248 pages • 33 b/w sketches • 5 1/2 x 8 1/4 • 0-7818-0715-8 • W • $14.95hc • (793)

Twenty Scottish Tales and Legends

Edited by Cyril Swinson

Illustrated by Allan Stewart

Twenty enchanting stories take the reader to an extraordinary world of magic harps, angry giants, mysterious spells and gallant Knights.

Ages 9 and up

215 pages • 5 1/2 x 8 1/4 • 8 b/w illustrations • 0-7818-0701-8 • W • $14.95 hc • (789)

Swedish Fairy Tales

Translated by H. L. Braekstad

A unique blending of enchantment, adventure, comedy, and romance make this collection of Swedish fairy tales a must-have for any library.

Ages 9 and up

190 pages • 21 b/w illustrations • 51/2 x 81/4 • 0-7818-0717-4 • W • $12.50hc • (787)

The Little Mermaid and Other Tales

Hans Christian Andersen

Here is a near replica of the first American edition of 27 classic fairy tales from the masterful Hans Christian Andersen.

Ages 9 and up

508 pages • b/w illustrations • 6 x 9 • 0-7818-0720-4 • W • $19.95hc • (791)

Pakistani Folk Tales: Toontoony Pie and Other Stories

Ashraf Siddiqui and Marilyn Lerch

Illustrated by Jan Fairservis

In these 22 folk tales are found not only the familiar figures of folklore—kings and beautiful princesses—but the magic of the Far East, cunning jackals, and wise holy men.

Ages 7 and up

158 pages • 6 1/2 x 8 1/2 • 38 illustrations • 0-7818-0703-4 • W • $12.50hc • (784)

Folk Tales from Chile

Brenda Hughes

This selection of 15 tales gives a taste of the variety of Chile's rich folklore. Fifteen charming illustrations accompany the text.

Ages 7 and up

121 pages • 5 1/2 x 8 1/4 • 15 illustrations • 0-7818-0712-3 • W • $12.50hc • (785)

All prices subject to change. **To purchase Hippocrene Books** contact your local bookstore, call (718) 454-2366, or write to: HIPPOCRENE BOOKS, 171 Madison Avenue, New York, NY 10016. Please enclose check or money order, adding $5.00 shipping (UPS) for the first book and $.50 for each additional book.